Preparing for Examinations 2

CONTENTS

ANALYSIS

From the overture 'The Thieving Magpie' (Rossini)

1. Name the key of this extract.

2. Using chord symbols, name the harmonies in bars 2, 4, 6 and 14.

3. Name the cadences and keys in bars 9-12 and 15-16.

4. Give the technical term which describes the relationship between bars 9 and 10 and bars 11 and 12.

5. Describe the 'unessential' (i.e. non-harmonic) notes in the melody at (a), (b), (c) and (d).

1. Name the key of this melody.

2. Name the cadences and keys in bars 2, 4, 8, 10, 20.

3. Give the bar numbers of three passages in the relative major.

4. The first musical idea appears in bars 1-2 in E minor and then in bars 3-4 in G major. Give two words to describe this device.

5. Give the bar numbers and keys of two other examples of this device.

6. What is the form of the tune?

From a 'Song without Words' (Mendelssohn)

Andante

(a)

(b)

(c)   (d)

1. Give the time-signature.

2. Give the meaning of *Andante*.

3. Describe the intervals between the highest and lowest notes at (a), (b), (c) and (d).

4. Name the cadence and key in bar 8.

5. In the passage from bar 11 to the first chord in bar 13:
   (a) what key does Mendelssohn lead us to expect?
   (b) into which key does he in fact go?

6. Write the tenor part of bars 1 and 2 in the appropriate C clef.

7. Using the correct key-signature, transpose the melody of bars 1 and 2 down a minor third.

8. Name the first and last notes foreign to the original key occurring in this extract.

9. Say in a few words why, in your opinion, Mendelssohn called the piece a 'Song without Words'.

10. Name the degrees of the scale (tonic, supertonic, etc.) of the first three notes of the melody.

From a piano solo by Samuel Arnold (1740-1802)

1. Give the time-signature.

2. Name the key of the extract.

3. Describe the modulation in bars 5-6.

4. Describe the triads used in the chords marked (a), (b), (c) and (d) as *major, minor* or *diminished.*

5. Name the intervals in the right-hand part at (e), (f), (g) and (h).

6. Write the left-hand part of bars 1-4 using the Alto C clef.

From 'Invitation to the Dance' (Weber)

1. Name the key in which this extract opens and the key in which it ends.

2. Using chord symbols, name the harmonies (one chord per bar) in bars 1-16 and indicate the modulations.

3. Name the auxiliary notes in bar 4.

4. Name the passing notes in bar 6.

5. Comment upon the relationship between melody and bass in bars 9-13.

6. Give a technical term to describe the first, third and sixth quavers of the melody in bar 17.

A chorale 'Jesu, meine Freude' (J.S. Bach)

1. Name the key of this chorale.

2. Give the time-signature.

3. Give the meaning of the sign ⌢.

4. Name the cadence in bar 4.

5. Name the keys in bar 8 and in bars 10-11 and state their relationships to the original key.

6. Describe the intervals between the soprano and alto parts at (a), (b), (c) and (d).

7. Write the tenor part of bars 1 and 2 using the Tenor C clef.

8. Using the correct key-signature, transpose the tenor part of bars 11-13 down a major third. (You may use the Tenor C clef if you prefer.)

9. The chorale ends with a perfect cadence. What is the technical name for the special effect used here and also at the end of the previous phrase?

10. Where is there an extended phrase?

11. Say briefly what is meant by the word 'chorale'.

From a piano piece 'Grandmother tells a ghost story' (op. 81) by Theodor Kullak (1818-82)

1. Name the key of this extract.

2. Give the time-signature.

3. Give the meaning of *allegretto* and *parlando.*

4. Name the intervals in the right-hand part at (a), (b), (c) and (d).

5. Give a technical term to describe the long sustained D in bars 1-3. What is the musical effect of this long note?

6. Why is the title appropriate?

7. Transcribe the melody of bars 1-4 for viola, using the appropriate C clef.

From a part-song (Mendelssohn)

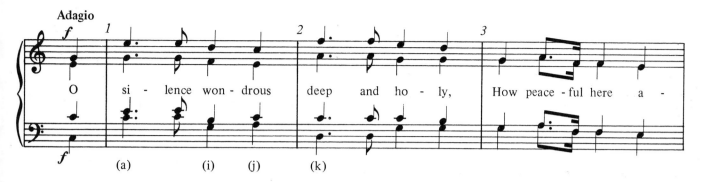

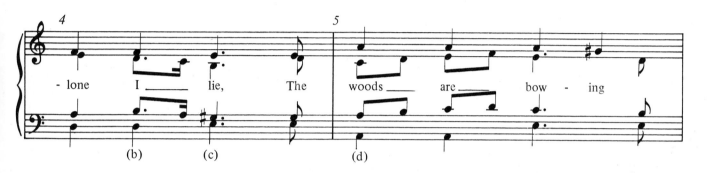

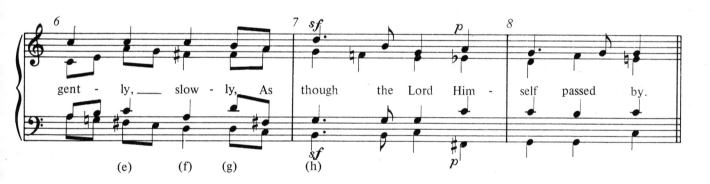

1. Give the time-signature.

2. Give the meaning of *adagio*.

3. Explain *sf*.

4. Describe each of the triads used in the chords marked (a), (b), (c) and (d) as *major, minor, augmented* or *diminished*.

5. Name the intervals between the tenor and bass parts at (e), (f), (g) and (h).

6. Name the degrees of the scale (*tonic, supertonic* etc.) used in the bass part at (i), (j) and (k).

7. Name the cadences and keys used in bars 4 and 8.

8. Write the tenor part of bars 3-4 in the Tenor C clef.

9. Explain how Mendelssohn has echoed the meaning of the words in his musical setting.

From 'Popular Song' in 'Album for the Young' (Schumann)

1. Name the key of this extract.

2. Give the time-signature.

3. Give the meaning of *lamentoso.*

4. Name the intervals of the right-hand part at (a), (b), (c), (d) and (e).

5. Describe each of the chords at (f), (g) and (h) as *major, minor, augmented* or *diminished.*

6. Give the bar numbers of examples of each of the following cadences: (a) Imperfect Cadence, (b) Interrupted Cadence.

7. Is the title 'Popular Song' appropriate? Give reasons for your answer.

From Symphony in G minor, K. 550 (Mozart)

1. Describe the structure of (a) bars 1-6; (b) bars 7-14.

2. Give one word to describe the relationship of melody between bars 1-2 and bars 3-4.

3. Identify the cadence at bars 13-14.

4. Where is the climax in this passage and how does Mozart build up to it?

5. Write a short paragraph on the importance of rests in music. Refer to this extract by way of illustration.

6. Give the date of the birth and death of Mozart and state in which country he lived.

7. Name (a) four compositions, including an opera and a symphony, by Mozart;
   (b) two composers contemporary with Mozart;
   (c) an historical event which took place during Mozart's lifetime.

From the opera 'Dido and Aeneas' (Purcell)

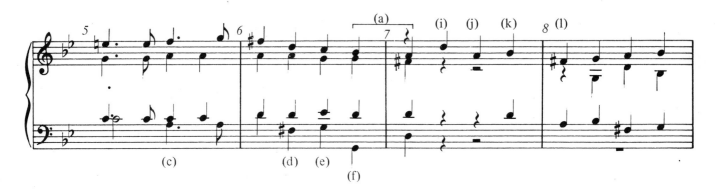

1. Give the time-signature.

2. Give the meaning of *andante maestoso*.

3. Name the cadences and keys at (a) and (b).

4. Name the intervals between tenor and bass at (c), (d), (e) and (f).

5. Name the degrees of the scale (tonic, supertonic, etc.) used in the soprano part at (i), (j), (k), and (l).

6. Write the tenor part of bars 7-9 in the Tenor C clef.

7. Describe each of the triads used in the chords marked (m), (n) and (o) as *major, minor* or *diminished*.

8. Describe the use of keys.

12

From Symphony in G minor, K. 550 (Mozart)

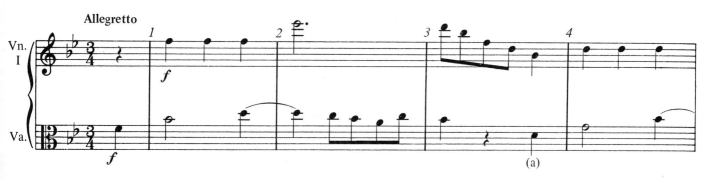

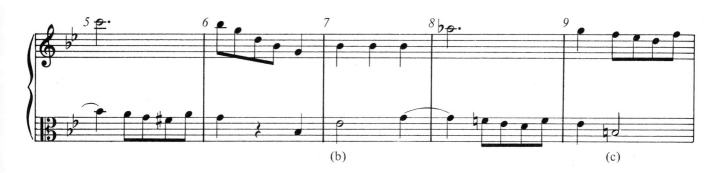

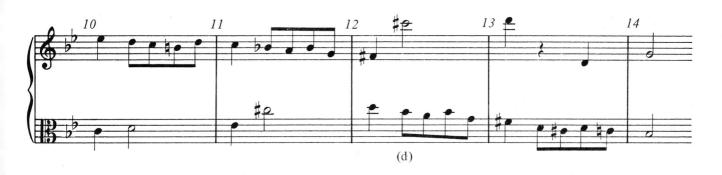

1. Rewrite the extract but use the G clef for the viola part.

2. In what key does the passage begin?

3. In what key does it end?

4. Trace the modulations between bar 3 (last beat) and bar 11 (first beat).

5. Name the intervals at (a), (b), (c) and (d).

6. What is the meaning of syncopation? How is it produced? Describe two kinds of syncopation to be found in the viola part.

7. Indicate the climax of the viola part.

8. What is the meaning of sequence? Give the bar numbers of any sequential passages.

9. Comment upon any features of the part-writing which you consider to be especially interesting.

From 'Christmas Oratorio' (J.S. Bach)

1. What is the key of the passage?

2. To what key does the music modulate in bars 5-6?

3. Point out an example of sequence in the voice part.

4. What is the meaning of imitation? Point out a passage where the accompaniment imitates the voice part.

5. Name the degrees of the scale (tonic, dominant, etc.) used in the voice part in bar 9.

6. Using chord symbols, describe the harmonies of the penultimate bar.

From Piano Sonata no. 10 in C (Haydn)

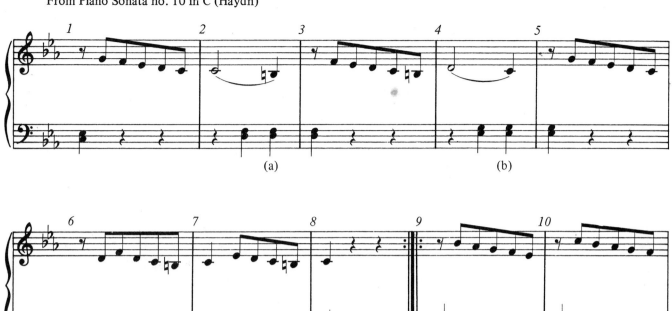

1. Give the time-signature.

2. The extract is taken from a dance movement. Suggest an appropriate title.

3. Describe the use of keys.

4. Describe each of the triads used in the chords marked (a), (b) and (c) as *major, minor* or *diminished.*

5. Name the ornament in the final bar. What should be played?

6. Comment upon the rhythm of the R.H. part in bars 12-14.

7. Comment upon the phrase structure in bars 9-15.

From Rondo in A minor, K. 511 (Mozart)

1. Name the key of this passage.

2. Name the ornaments within the brackets in bars 1 and 7.

3. Rewrite the melody in bar 7 showing how the ornament should be played.

4. Indicate
   (a) two cadential $^6_4$'s;
   (b) an imperfect cadence;
   (c) a perfect cadence;
   (d) a lower auxiliary note;
   (e) a tonic pedal;
   (f) a descending melodic minor scale;
   (g) an appoggiatura in bar 6;
   (h) a dominant seventh in root position.

5. Analyse the harmony in bar 4.

Hornpipe in E minor (Purcell)

1. Give the time-signature.

2. Write down the rhythmic motif which dominates the R.H. part.

3. Explain syncopation and give two examples from the Hornpipe.

4. Explain melodic inversion and give two examples from the Hornpipe.

5. Give the bar numbers of a passage in the relative major.

6. Explain (a) ⌐1⌐

     (b) ‖: :‖

     (c) ⌢

7. Point out thematic links between the R.H. and L.H. parts of bars 1-3.

From Piano Concerto in A minor (Schumann)

1. Give the time-signature.

2. Name the key of this passage.

3. What key is suggested by the chords in bars 3-5?

4. What key is suggested by the chords in bars 6-7?

5. Describe each of the chords used in bars 1, 6, 7, 8 and 11 as *major, minor, dominant seventh* or *diminished seventh.*

6. Point out an example of a dominant pedal.

7. Name the intervals within the brackets at (x), (y) and (z).

18

From the overture to the opera 'Oberon' (Weber)

1. Name six appoggiaturas in the melody of bars 1 and 2.

2. Using chord symbols, name the harmonies in bars 1-4 and bars 7, 8, 10 and 11.

3. Write out the three diminished sevenths used in bars 5 and 6 putting the 'sharpest' note at the bottom of each chord, (i.e. the first one will be written as

4. Write out the diminished seventh that the sequential movement leads us to expect on the first beat of bar 7.

From 'Harold in Italy' (Berlioz)

20

The cor anglais is a transposing instrument and its notes sound a perfect fifth lower than written.

1. Rewrite the extract, transposing the cor anglais part down a perfect fifth, and complete the piano accompaniment keeping up the quaver pattern established in bars 1-3. The small notes in the R.H. part indicate the harmonies to be used.

2. Using chord symbols, name the harmonies in bars 4, 5, 6, 7 and 9. Set out your answer in such a way that it shows how modulation is brought about by means of a pivot chord.

3. Name the cadence formed by bars 7 and 9.
   How do you explain the harmony in bar 8?

4. Write each of the chords on the first beats of bars 10 and 13 in root position on the treble stave.

5. The cor anglais melody does not fall into regular four-bar phrases. Explain the structure of the melody.

6. The extract comes from the third movement of Berlioz's 'Harold in Italy'. This is entitled 'The Serenade of a Mountaineer of the Abruzzi to his Mistress'. Is the title appropriate? Give reasons for your answer.

7. Name another orchestral instrument which sounds a perfect fifth below its written notes.

From Divertimento in B flat, K. Anh. 229/II (Mozart)

Rewrite the passage on two staves, using G and F clefs.

22

1. In what key does the extract begin and end?

2. To what key does the music modulate in bars 5-8?

3. Describe the chords at (a), (b), (c), (d), (e) and (f) using chord symbols or figured bass notation.

4. Name the cadences in bars 7-8 and 11-12.

5. Point out a passage involving imitation between clarinets and bassoon.

6. Point out a passage involving imitation by inversion between the two clarinets.

7. Give a brief description of Simple Rondo form.

From Cello Concerto, op. 104 (Dvořák)

Rewrite the extract a semitone lower in the key of G sharp minor (the original key). Write the cello part in the Tenor C clef.

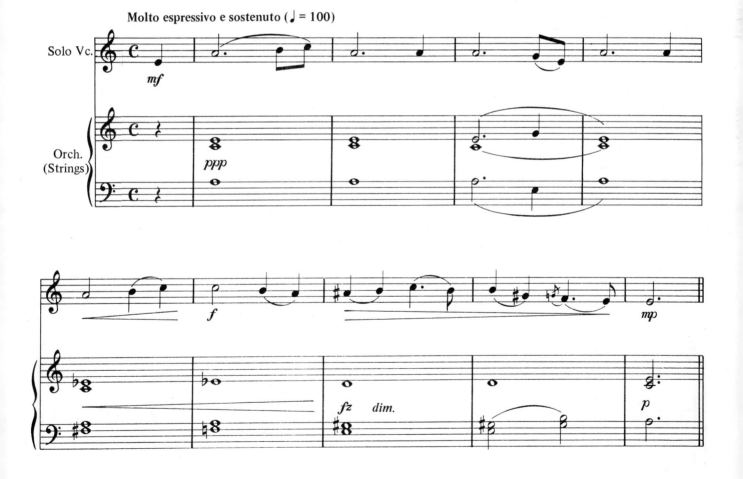

From Symphony no. 8 in G, op. 88 (Dvořák)

1. Beginning as follows, rewrite the extract on two staves as for piano.

Allegro con brio

When you have completed your arrangement play it through a number of times until you are thoroughly familiar with the sound of Dvořák's harmonies.

2. In what key does the music begin?

3. In what key does it end?

4. Name the cadence and key at bars 10-11 and 15-18.

5. Identify the scale upon which the melody of bars 1-6 is based.

6. Name the intervals that occur between Trombones I and II in bars 15-17.

7. Dvořák has not written a 16-bar sentence (4 + 4 + 4 + 4). Give the length of the phrases that make up this 18-bar extract.

8. Write a short appreciation of the extract commenting upon features of melody, harmony, mood and style.

Ayre in D minor (Purcell)

1. Write down the rhythmic motif that dominates the right-hand part.

2. Give the bar numbers of the passage in the relative major key.

3. Using chord symbols, describe the harmonies from bar 9 to the end.

4. Point out a passage in the left-hand part which uses the melodic minor scale.

5. Complete the following variations maintaining the style of Purcell's *Ayre in D minor*.

PIANO ACCOMPANIMENTS

Complete the following accompaniments developing the ideas contained in the given parts.

3 **Allegro moderato**

O, the noble Duke of York

Andante

Swing low, sweet chariot

5 **Allegro**

A French folksong

A German Dance
(Schubert)

6   Walzer

V7 in F _____

I in F   I   V7c   Ib   Ic in C _____ V7   I
         ⌐ in D minor ⌐

31

Con spirito

A negro spiritual: Steal away

Andante con moto

Steal a-way, steal a-way, steal a-way to Je-sus! Steal a-way, steal a-way home, I

poco più mosso

hain't got long to stay here. My Lord — he calls — me, He calls me by the

rall.

thun-der; The trumpet sounds with-in-a my soul, I hain't got long to stay here.

Con moto

10 Moderato

English folksong: As I was a-walking

Gmin.　　　C

F　　　Gmin.　　Dmin.　　Dmin.　　C7　　F　　Amin.

B♭　　　F　　　Dmin.　　Gmin.　　Dmin

Aeolian mode (transposed)

The chords you will use;

Dmin.　　　F　Gmin. Amin. B♭　C　Dmin.

11 Con moto

My bonny lies over the ocean

I IV I _____ VI V7 _____

IIb V7

V7d

cresc.

12 Espressivo

Tom's gone to Hilo

Broken chords

Many songs have a rippling accompaniment in which there is an uninterrupted flow of quavers or semiquavers based upon broken chords. Sometimes the opening pattern is kept up throughout the song but more often than not there is a measure of flexibility. This may be achieved by transferring a pattern from one hand to the other and by introducing occasional touches of counterpoint as in the following accompaniment to 'Maa Bonny Lad'.

1   **Andante espressivo**   Northumbrian folksong

1. Hev ye seen owt o' maa bon-ny lad, And are ye sure he's weel oh! He's
2. Yes, aa've seen your bon-ny lad, Up - on the sea aa spied him. His

gyen o - wer land wiv his stick in his hand, He's gyen to moor the keel, oh.
grave is green but not wi' grass; Thou'lt ne - ver lie a - side him.

Write flowing accompaniments to the following melodies.

2 Andante cantabile   Plaisir d'amour (Martini)

3 Andantino   An air by Paisiello

4　Andante espressivo　　　　　　　　　　　　　　　　　　Ye banks and braes

Fine

5　Dolce　　　　　　　　　　　　　　　　　　　　　Flow gently, sweet Afton

Con ped.

I　　　　　　　　　　Ib　　　　IV　　V7　　　　　　　I

V7 in B♭　　　　　　　I in B♭　　　　♮IV7 in F　　　　V7

I　　　　　　　　　　Ib　　　　IV　　V7　　　　　　　I

In varied styles

1 Allegretto grazioso

Sweet nightingale

Notice this important motif:

Introduce it into your accompaniment at some point as a foil to the rhythmic idea of bars 1-6.

4   **Con spirito** A French marching song

F minor: V _____ I   E♭ major V _____ I

Andante sostenuto

A Scottish cradle song

O! can ye sew cush - ions, and can ye sew sheets? And can ye sing ba - la - low when the bairn greets? And hee and baw, bird - ie, and hee and baw, lamb, And hee and baw, bird - ie, my bon - nie wee lamb.

Con spirito

HISTORY OF MUSIC

(Checklists of Topics and Composers)

1550 - 1650

Topics

Polyphony	Variations	Organ
Mass	Fantasia (Fancy)	Virginals
Motet	Pavan and Galliard	Clavichord
Madrigal	Alman (Allemande)	Harpsichord
Ballett	Coranto (Courante)	Viols
Chanson	Jig (Gigue)	Recorders
Canzonet	Canzona	Cornetts
Lute-song	Ricercar	Sackbuts
The Triumphs	*The Fitzwilliam*	Consort Music
of Oriana	*Virginal Book*	

Composers

Tallis	(1505 - 85)	Sweelinck	(1562 - 1621)
Gabrieli, A.	(*c.*1510 - 86)	Dowland	(*c.*1563 - 1626)
Palestrina	(1525 - 94)	Farnaby	(*c.*1565 - 1640)
Lassus	(1532 - 94)	Monteverdi	(1567 - 1643)
Byrd	(1543 - 1623)	Tomkins	(1572 - 1656)
Marenzio	(1553 - 99)	Gibbons	(1583 - 1625)
Morley	(1557 - *c.*1603)	Frescobaldi	(1583 - 1643)
Gabrieli, G.	(1557 - 1612)	Schütz	(1585 - 1672)
Bull	(1563 - 1628)	Froberger	(1616 - 67)

1600 - 1750

Topics

Variations	Passacaglia: Chaconne	Passion Music
Suite: Partita	Ground bass: Ostinato	Chorale
Ordre: Lesson	Violin: violin makers	Cantata
Orchestral Suite	Opera	Service
Concerto Grosso	Monody	Anthem
Solo Concerto	Continuo	Fugue
Solo Sonata	Recitative	*The Beggar's Opera*
Sonata da chiesa	Oratorio	*The English*
Sonata da camera	Masque	*Dancing Master*

Composers

Peri	(1561 - *c.*1633)	Purcell	(1659 - 95)
Monteverdi	(1567 - 1643)	Scarlatti, A.	(1660 - 1725)
Schutz	(1585 - 1672)	Kuhnau	(1660 - 1722)
Lawes H.	(1596 - 1662)	Couperin	(1668 - 1733)
Cavalli	(1602 - 76)	Vivaldi	(1678 - 1741)
Carissimi	(1605 - 74)	Geminiani	(1680 - 1762)
Lully	(1633 - 87)	Telemann	(1681 - 1767)
Buxtehude	(1637 - 1707)	Rameau	(1683 - 1764)
Blow	(1648 - 1708)	Bach, J. S.	(1685 - 1750)
Pachelbel	(1653 - 1706)	Handel	(1685 - 1759)
Corelli	(1653 - 1713)	Scarlatti, D.	(1685 - 1757)

1725 - 1830

Topics

Sonata form	*Style galant*	Opera
Symphony	Fortepiano	Opera buffa
Divertimento	Clavecin	Oratorio
Serenade	Mannheim School	Mass
Sonata	Mannheim Orchestra	Requiem
Quartet		Lied
Concerto		Song cycle

Composers

Couperin	(1668 - 1733)	Stamitz, J.	(1717 - 57)
Sammartini, G. B.	(1698 - 1775)	Haydn, J.	(1732 - 1809)
Pergolesi	(1710 - 36)	Bach, J. C.	(1735 - 82)
Bach, W. F.	(1710 - 84)	Mozart	(1756 - 91)
Bach, C. P. E.	(1714 - 88)	Beethoven	(1770 - 1827)
Gluck	(1714 - 87)	Schubert	(1797 - 1828)

1820 - 1900

Topics

Symphony	The piano	Songs	Oratorio
Symphonic poem	and its music	without words	Mass
Overture	Prelude	Humoresque	Requiem
Concerto	Etude	Romance	Opera
Sonata	Rhapsody	Fantasia	Music-drama
Quartet	Ballade	Lyric pieces	Operetta
Programme music	Nocturne	Album leaf	Lied
Nationalism	Impromptu	Duets	Song cycle
	Dances		

Composers

Beethoven	(1770-1827)	Bizet	(1838 - 75)
Weber	(1786-1826)	Mussorgsky	(1839 - 81)
Schubert	(1797 - 1828)	Borodin	(1833 - 87)
Berlioz	(1803 - 69)	Brahms	(1833 - 97)
Strauss, J.	(1804 - 49)	Balakirev	(1837 - 1910)
Glinka	(1804 - 57)	Tchaikovsky	(1840 - 93)
Mendelssohn	(1809 - 47)	Dvořák	(1841 - 1904)
Chopin	(1810 - 49)	Sullivan	(1842 - 1900)
Schumann	(1810 - 56)	Grieg	(1843 - 1907)
Liszt	(1811 - 86)	Rimsky-Korsakov	(1844 - 1908)
Wagner	(1813 - 83)	Fauré	(1845 - 1924)
Verdi	(1813 - 1901)	Janacek	(1854 - 1928)
Offenbach	(1819 - 80)	Wolf	(1860 - 1903)
Franck	(1822 - 90)	Mahler	(1860 - 1911)
Smetana	(1824 - 84)	German	(1862 - 1936)
Bruckner	(1824 - 96)	Strauss, R.	(1864 - 1949)

1890 to the present day

Topics

Impressionism	Song	Orchestra
Whole-tone scale	Symphony	Neo-classicism
Pentatonic scale	Symphonic poem	Folk music
Modes	Sonata	Serial composition
Harmonic developments	Quartet	Musique concrète
Chromaticism	Concerto	Aleatory music
Atonality	Piano	Notation
Opera	Ballet	Electronic music
Oratorio		Broadcasting
Mass		Recording

Composers

Elgar	(1857 - 1934)	Kodály	(1882 - 1967)
Puccini	(1858 - 1924)	Stravinsky	(1882 - 1971)
Mahler	(1860 - 1911)	Webern	(1883 - 1945)
Debussy	(1862 - 1918)	Berg	(1885 - 1935)
Delius	(1862 - 1934)	Varèse	(1885 - 1965)
Strauss	(1864 - 1949)	Prokofiev	(1891 - 1953)
Nielsen	(1865 - 1931)	Hindemith	(1895 - 1963)
Sibelius	(1865 - 1957)	Poulenc	(1899 - 1963)
Vaughan Williams	(1872 - 1958)	Copland	(1900 -
Rachmaninov	(1873 - 1943)	Walton	(1902 -
Holst	(1874 - 1934)	Dallapiccola	(1905 - 78)
Schoenberg	(1874 - 1951)	Tippett	(1905 -
Ives	(1874 - 1954)	Shostakovich	(1906 - 75)
Ravel	(1875 - 1937)	Messiaen	(1908 -
Falla	(1876 - 1946)	Britten	(1913 - 76)
Ireland	(1879 - 1962)	Boulez	(1925 -
Bartók	(1881 - 1945)	Stockhausen	(1928 -